PRAISE FOR
Z is for Zapatazo

Rivera's poems remind that the "spaces between what America says it is and what it is" are myriad, lived in, and leave their mark. The school room, the family home, the interpersonal encounters between whiteness and brownness, the barrio, the place of contact between Latinx social experience and the comic book or television program or pulp fiction, the memories called up by a photograph – from within these inhabited spaces Rivera finds a voice that calls for a world to match its words.

- Bruce Campbell, *̶̶̶̶̶ ̶fessor of Hispanic Studies, Dir. Latino/Latin An̶ ̶ ̶s, College of Saint Benedict & Saint John's Uni̶ ̶*

Ruben Rivera is a poet ̶ ̶ ̶ ̶ ̶rise from the heart to become unforgettable poems sing ̶ ̶ ̶us to listen. When we do, we discover that his rhythm̶ ̶ ̶rough the language of poetry we have been seeking. V̶ ̶ ̶he poet and the reader arrive together, these wonderfu̶ ̶ ̶be waiting.

- Ramon Gonzale̶ ̶ ̶ ̶*of English, University of Minnesota, award-w̶ ̶ ̶or of ten books of poetry, including* The Hea̶ ̶ ̶ ̶ ̶vals *and* The Religion of Hands. *Ramon has edited a dozen anthologies, served as Poetry Editor of the* Bloomsbury Review *since 1980, and received a Lifetime Achievement Award in Literature from the Border Regional Library Association.*

Lyrical, vivid and heartfelt, *Z is for Zapatazo* announces Ruben Rivera's prodigious talents. This debut collection covers a lifetime of experiences from childhood challenges to visions of heaven, with memoir-like poems offering insights into what it means to be a Nuyorican or a homeboy growing up in racialized America. Other poems muse on spiritual connections to people and earth. New and original, his clarion voice is a gift for the reader.

- Angela Shannon, *Associate Professor of English at Bethel University in Minnesota and author of* Singing the Bones Together.

is for Zapatazo

RUBEN RIVERA

Z is for Zapatazo

POEMS BETWEEN THE SPACES

atmosphere press

© 2022 Ruben Rivera

Published by Atmosphere Press

Cover design by Ronaldo Alves

No part of this book may be reproduced without permission from the author except in brief quotations and in reviews.

atmospherepress.com

For Anita Pelayo Rivera. Her father, José, fled Mexico to California during the wars of the Mexican Revolution. At 5 years, all adult males in his family were hidden under a pile of corn to escape conscription-or-death from Pancho Villa's army, while Villa's horses ate the corn. He lived to see Haley's Comet twice. He married Grace and they bore a daughter, my wife of 40 years and if everyone was like her war would simply not occur to anyone.

None of the poems and prose pieces in this collection have been previously published. I have never tried to publish them until now. However, several have won awards. Miss Rice won 2d place in New Hampshire's 2021 MacGregor Poetry contest. Isolde, Prayer for Nothing, The Gospel of Bulldog, Of Parts and Partings, How to Quit Smoking, In the Beginning, Who Sinned?, Black Hole, Birdman, and Quadrennial won League of Minnesota Poets awards during three years when I was a member and submitted a few poems to their annual contest.

CONTENTS

1. In the Beginning

The Palsy 3

Miss Rice 4

In the beginning 6

Z is for Zapatazo 7

Birdman 10

The Gemcutter 11

The Fall of Middle Earth 12

Great White Sharks 13

Black Hole 14

How I started hating conspiracy theories 15

Last Voyage of the Gemcutter 16

2. Duck and Cover

Prayer to Galactus 19

Duck and Cover 20

un-earthed manuscript remarkably preserved except ending 21

I Don't Mean 22

The Poet 24

The Monuments Version 26
Lazrus 27
Rogue 29
Lines 30
for those who hate blm but claim they would have loved mlk 1 32
quadrennial 33
for those who hate blm but claim they would have loved mlk 2 34
El Paso and Dayton 35
for those who hate blm but claim they would have loved mlk 3 36
Prayer for Nothing 37

3. Vatos

Vatos 41

4. Seasonal Affective Disorder

Seasonal Affective Disorder 53
Special Relativity 54
Where is Everybody? 55
How to quit smoking 56
American Sentences 58
The Bad News 59

Who Sinned? 60
College Diner 61
The Plunge 62
The Gospel of Bulldog 63
Pulp Fiction Women 64
Final Frontier 66
If obituaries told all 67

5. Heaven is Other People

Of Faith and Things Seen 71
Shalom 73
Anniversarium[31] 74
That time of year 75
When I was a Child 76
Isolde 78
Dawning 80
Heaven is Other People 81
Sachem 83
Of Parts and Partings 85

1. IN THE BEGINNING

The Palsy

In the picture she looks pensive,
       with one side of her mouth drawn permanently
              downward from a childhood palsy,

according to family lore,
       the result of plunging into cold water
              in the heat of summer.

She is sitting on one of those chairs that looks
       like it belonged in Disney's House of the Future,
              or a rocket to Mars, whichever came first.

Everything in the Gotham tenement is boxy,
       black and white, far from the Dali-like tropical
              rhapsody of her beloved *Boriquén*.

She is cinched in that ubiquitous rayon housedress
       that TV moms wore as if expecting to be dined out, but
              she was just expecting.

She is so young, all her edges velvet,
       not yet worn by the patriarchal obligations
              of virginal motherhood. My father is not

in the
       picture,
              only

stayed long enough to be in one, the wedding:
       she leans on him, head at an amorous angle
              like a movie star, her face pensive,

with one side of her mouth drawn permanently
       downward, the result of plunging into cold water
              in the heat of summer.

Miss Rice

You resembled water seeking the best path
through the hot, compacted asphalt
that was school, and the chain-linked recess lot studded
with tether ball poles, and dodge ball rings,
hop-scotch blocks, merry-go-rounds, swings and slides,
the ground flattened to the consistency of cement
from years of trampling Keds and Buster Browns
so that rain had to find other paths – between
the Quonset hut classrooms where sewer grates
led to the concrete highway of the Los Angeles River –
and finally arrived at the sea in a state that resembled
sudsy beer and digested corn-nuts.

You trickled through hallways lined with lockers,
padlocks hanging like forbidden fruit, past young bucks,
proud freshly hung testicles and stubbled antlers,
competing for the most forbidden fruit of all, and
that other contest, the one to see who cared less
about anything, the winners crowned cool. You floated in

with your cart of books and lesson plans and dreams
of improving the world, clothes crisp, girly,
right out of Sears & Roebuck, hair in a beehive,
feet in heels and still just under five
feet tall, skin shimmering like a newly-washed baby,
plump and poreless. Your face The Pietà, child-bride
and mother of all suffering. You were perfect.

We were the scared ones. For all our toughness,
ever conforming to prove our non-conformity,
and bewildered by a butterfly in a meadow fluttering
over wisps of nectar none of us could can.
You loved us, really loved us, and suffered
the suffering of unrequited love. By God

people can be such perfect bastards.
In Plato's realm of Forms we were the models
for all inferior bastardry in this imperfect world. Was it

when we jacked the projector
and tied the film into knots? Or the tsunami
of interruptions, the darts of foul language?
Was it when we turned your classroom into a boxing
arena, or when we lit that desk on fire? Personally,

I think you endured until you came to class
and saw that huge nut-threaded bolt on your desk.
I think that wounded your heart more than any
thing. And I, I can say that I didn't do any of that.
You just stopped coming one day, and I didn't do
anything. You were perfect as spring rain. We
the hard ground that sewered you to sea.

In the beginning

there was a house to live in, and clothes
to wear to school, a sack lunch waiting
daily by the door like a faithful dog.
Dad would rise before anyone, switch off
the night, and complete the same tasks
before leaving for the diner: shower, shave,
put on his uniform, drink coffee... On cold days,
after he left, we competed for the bathroom,
warm and steaming of Old Spice.

A weathered Chevy that always ran, a doctor
who knew what was wrong with my ear,
a silhouette of presents under a tree.
He came home each day, resplendent
in his chocolate skin and chef whites and smile,
like the Cream of Wheat man, so happy
just to hand out another bowl of life-giving
mush to the children of the world.

A pitcher with wild flowers on the table
for mom and the house smelling like
Easter, or Castilian roses, harbinger
of the blessed virgin, to whom he prayed,
Hail Marys, Our Fathers, Acts of Contrition,
pinching bead after bead between resolute
thumb and forefinger and shuttling them
like sums on an abacus.

Boxed fried chicken from the diner,
and tubs of tapioca scooped,
trembling, into heavy bowls and dusted
with cinnamon, waxed paper wrapped
Armenian sandwiches the size of manhole covers,
beef Stroganoff, lemon pie. In the beginning
these things were miraculous as creation.
And what did a child know,
what did a child know,
of the costs of creating miracles?

       (With thanks to Robert Hayden)

Z is for Zapatazo

I started learning my ABC's before I could even read. The first lesson involved a woman collapsed in the back lot of the Bronx tenement where we lived. Something had scared her nearly to death. There in the pouring rain she lay writhing and screaming out her wits while neighbors watched from the covered balconies and fire escapes. R is for Rat.

Another lesson was connected to chickens in that time when "children should be seen and not heard." The Spanish version had, as usual, more syllables as well as color: "*Los niños hablan cuando las gallinas mean.*" "Children talk when the chickens pee." Those who relate to chicken only in conveniently dismembered extra crispy form may ask when or how often do chickens pee? Never. We Nuyoricans, Spanglish-speaking Gothamites, who had never seen a chicken except when it arrived steaming aromatically on a plate with rice and beans, nevertheless knew well that chickens don't relieve themselves like little boys and girls. C is for Chickens.

We moved to California, that hub of social contradictions. There I was raised on breezy primetime shows, punctuated by interruptions about some protest march, police suppression, riot, space-race launch, cold war threat, assassination, or other scary event. For a while it seemed like "We Interrupt This Program" was part of the regular TV line up. Maybe that's why there were so many sitcoms and family shows – diversions from the worry and sheer terror. The shows conveyed placid American suburbs lined with houses that never needed painting, populated by families like the Andersons, the Nelsons, and the Cleavers, lovingly and rationally ruled by parents that never yelled or hit or even had sex.

Meanwhile, on this side of the fourth wall, verbal and physical discipline was natural. So natural in fact that it was conveyed in a Spanish-language ABC book for children. The benign English version that the Cleavers read had, "A is for Apple, B is for Ball, C is for Cat" and so on, to the last letter, "Z is for Zoo." A logical entry for the Spanish *Zeta* (Z) would have been *Zapato* (Shoe), something every Latino child would know. But instead it read, *"Z es por Zapatazo"* (paraphrased: Z is for Shoe Missile). The expounded letter was accompanied by a drawing of a dark-haired child with its wincing face cocked to the side from the impact of a flying shoe. A friend recalled the book to me years later and we responded with equal parts laughter and loathing at the kind of mentality that would include such a casually violent lesson in what is perhaps the most basic childhood introduction to an intelligible world.

History reminds me, however, that Anglo American ways of child rearing were not so idyllic as the TV shows portrayed. In colonial New England, a child's education went hand in hand with physical discipline. The 1691 edition of *The New England Primer* for children had ABC lessons that included: "F: The idle FOOL is whipt at school," and "J: JOB feels the rod, yet blesses God." And even as the belt-free world of "Father Knows Best" and "Leave It To Beaver" was being beamed into televisions across North America, teachers in schools who looked just like Robert Young and Barbara Billingsley blistered our tender behinds with every device imaginable, from ping pong paddles to a cricket bat perforated in wood shop by one particularly sadistic misanthrope to cut wind resistance.

I can at least affirm that I advanced in my ABC's fairly early in the game – my older brother, not so much. If I say that too frequently I followed a crowd of kids to an afterschool fight only to discover that my brother was one of the young gladiators, you'll understand what I mean. The same feckless pugnacity repeatedly got him into needless trouble at home, where there was no immunity of non-combatants. K is for Knucklehead.

Years later, my mom and stepdad divorced. (My birth father I knew only through an old wedding photograph and mom's spectacularly imaginative comparisons to our misbehavior.) By then I was married, living at the other end of the country and going to seminary. I did not know the degree to which their split had affected me. Then one evening, after my wife had gone to bed and I stayed up studying, I sank into an abyss of grief, crying and shaking uncontrollably.

Gone were the family parties when we kids listened to music and played while our parents did…whatever parents did at parties, until the sensuous Puerto Rican food appeared miraculously on the table to be gobbled up by gangly calorie-burning urchins, leaving the mess to be cleaned up by elves while we slept soundly wherever our bodies happened to land. Gone was the Monorail, and the Matterhorn, It's A Small World, and the Adventure Thru Inner Space courtesy of Monsanto. Gone Knott's berry pie. Gone the excursions to Pacific Ocean Park, Redondo Beach, and Newport Dunes, the broiling burgers, the quenching watermelon.

Gone the chilly early hours of Christmas when we'd sneak out of our beds to peek at the gift-wrapped silhouettes under the tree and imagine they were what we wanted. Gone a mother's tender ministrations when any of us kids were sick. Gone her tears when she saw mine after a broken wrist ended high school gymnastics. Gone the rosary prayer circles and sleepless nights when my brother was in hospital with brain tumors. Gone the frantic calling for my sister lost in a Tijuana bazaar. Gone the tears of joy when she was found. Gone the dreaded daily tablespoon of cod liver oil and the sting of Mercurochrome on scraped knees and elbows.

Gone dad's brutal six-day workweek that underwrote our lives. Gone when the family sat around the only television in the house after eating dinner at the same table, at the same time, and the wild symphony of everyone talking at once. Gone the laughter, I'm talking Puerto Rican laughter, the world series of laughter, now only faint bells in the distant steeple of my memory. Z is for Zapatazo.

Birdman

He pestered for a parakeet and waxed on them
incessantly. But no one said no as much nor meant it
like our parents, the Guinness Record holders of no.
There we were again after school at the back of the store
that sold everything from penny candy to animals, me
staring at the monkey, fascinated, not so much by it,
but by what in the hell a monkey was doing in a five &
dime, my brother with the birds, mesmerized by something
I could not fathom. In truth,

I never understood his obsession with obsessions.
Without warning, he opened the cage, grabbed
a turquoise-feathered specimen, stuffed it head first
into one of the pockets of his Levi's, and
started-walking-across-the-entire-length-of-the-store-to-the-exit,
the infernal fowl yowling like a gagged kidnap victim,
which, I suppose, it was. He shouldn't have gotten away
with it, then or when we got home and he exclaimed:
"Mom, look what we found."

The Gemcutter

I used to imagine I was on a long Odyssean adventure. I sailed
on a trireme built of oaken hull over sturdy pine backbone
and ribs, an anatomy to endure the phalanx of swells sent
by the tyrant Sea. The rigging was rope made from papyrus
and flax fibers, the like once used to haul the stones for
pyramids and sphinxes. It was certainly strong enough
for the halyard in my hand that tamed the bleached white
sails swollen like pride in the wind.

I called my ship the Gemcutter. Its bow split the emerald sea,
cleaving a corridor of hissing foam and sped me
through dangers, to one marvel and another, until at last,
transfigured by the journey, I reached that ultimate destination
where my love awaited, my kin and crown.

Those were times when I was completely lost
in my head, imagination stronger than the laws
that sought to bind me to physical universe, stronger
even than fate always seeking to wrest the tiller
from my brined and calloused hands,
but not as strong as mom
yelling from the kitchen window
asking what was taking me
so long to hang the laundry.

The Fall of Middle Earth

One day, I went to that land
between home and school, shocked
to find it invaded. The scene
looked like a horde of dragons,
their plated skin clattering,
their movement stuttering
like some Harryhausean nightmare,
and generals commanding troops
in white helmets from blue paper
battle plans. The noise
cracked the sky's thin blue shell
and soot from organ pipe nostrils
nearly blocked out the running yolk
of the sun. Mandibles dropped open
dripping an earthy stew
then clammed shut with the metallic
squeal of lightning, like colossal
hinges on the gates of Mordor,
maws of these steel-veined horrors
engorging and disgorging
dirt, rocks, grasses, trees,
nests, warrens, dens and cloisters,
secret gardens, fens and shires.
Fangorn, Moria, Rivendell...

Great White Sharks

Our friends could see us coming
from a week away and the grief we endured
would have touched Job. My brother and I tried
to color them black with roll-on polish.
But the fiendish things kept absorbing it,
succeeding only in looking like
a bad Earl Scheib paint job.

Tried everything to shorten their life:
dragging our feet, scraping curbs and stones,
kicking trees, casting spells. These were the days

before kids had money and the occasional dime
or quarter was like finding Treasure Island. So I get it.
Our parents couldn't afford latest styles, and
things had to last. But was it too much to ask
that my shoes not look like great white sharks?

Black Hole

"...nor did I enjoy the thing for which I did the wrong, but the act of doing wrong itself."   Augustine, *Confessions*, Book II

According to Einstein every thing in the universe
puts a dent in space-time. But nothing did it
quite like our personal Boo Radley that
lived at the end of the block. Oh,
how we tortured him, and oh,
how he saved us. For here
I am decades later still
thinking about him,
filthy, scabby,
incubus of our
imaginings
from which
no light
could
escape,
here
I am
haran-
guing
hea-
ven
for
for-
give
n
e
s
s
.

How I started hating conspiracy theories

How often the truth is just not sexy enough. But the lie? Now that's an orgy.

In the fifth grade I caught the flu so bad I missed two weeks of school. When I returned my teacher got down on one knee to look me in the eyes and said: "Ruben, are you OK? I heard you got in trouble with the law and went to juvenile detention." "Home with the flu," I said. "Nearly died. Didn't you get mom's letter?" "I heard you were really in juvie." "Nope. Home sick. Nearly died." He walked away disappointed, in the same way dogs find catching cars disappointing. That year I was "Juvie Rubie," hang all my protestations for truth. Even today, I'm Juvie Rubie.

Last Voyage of the Gemcutter

I used to imagine I was on a long Odyssean adventure.
But all adventures end, and I was tired, long away
and far from home. The boat was agile sure, weatherly,
and served me well through one danger and another, but
could not last against ever-feuding wind and wave screaming
through the windows and blacking out the sun, tearing
the sails, and scudding my little boat like so much flotsam
on the last day mom and dad lived together.

2. DUCK AND COVER

For those who endure one zapatazo after another in the spaces between what America says it is and what it is, and help advance the grand, unfinished experiment.

Prayer to Galactus

Legendary comic book writer Stan Lee
told legendary comic book artist Jack Kirby
that he wanted the Fantastic Four to "fight god,"
and lo great Galactus was born, even had
a big "G" on his chest, then promptly thwarted
in the next issue. The Silver Surfer, gleaming rider
of the stellar spaceways, wielder of the power cosmic,
and herald to Galactus, devourer of worlds, betrayed
his master and helped the FF save Earth, to which
he was exiled as punishment, this world that could be
paradise, he lamented with tears extraterrestrial,
if we but learned the power of love. The Silver one
saved us from a god but could not save us
from ourselves. I should have seen that part
of the story. But I was barely ten
when Earth 616 was roiled by nuclear standoffs,
civil rights protests, police suppressions,
antiwar marches, police suppressions, riots,
police suppressions, assassinations. *We interrupt
this program* became part of the TV lineup. The world
needed superheroes, and I prayed earnestly
to become one. *God, you said
that whoever really believes can move mountains.
Then grant me super powers and I shall do just that –
bring peace on earth.* But the superhero world
is Manichean, Good and Evil always existing,
neither one omniscient, neither omnipotent – existing
in an ocean without personality, that cannot listen
and cannot answer – one never able to cancel the other,
one unable to exist without the other, all wins
never permanent, all defeats never complete. All this
is great for comic books, but for worlds
not so much. Prayers unanswered, my religion urged me
to depend on the power of love. But a ten-year old
still wonders if super powers might be more handy.

Duck and Cover

In the middle of cursive writing
practice so we could all write neat
as *Coca-Cola*, or that worn tale
about little George Washington
and the cherry tree, or a foray
into the New Math designed
to help us outsmart the reds,
without warning teacher would switch
the lights off and on furiously. In a flash
we dashed under our little desks
and covered our little heads
with our little hands, giggling,
the whole thing pointless
should a small sun visit school
for show and tell. Glaring down
on our crumb on the cosmic sleeve
was the same nuclear fire
worshipped by our ancestors,
no longer far enough away
to appear divinely benign. And still,
we giggled. Still, at recess we played
under that cold and callous sky,
cliques cliquing and
jocks jocking like normal. Still,
Ray bragged how he got to peek
up Lisa's dress during the drills. Still,
the feckless toughs who hated integration
ran by elementary school
throwing rocks through windows
and shouting, *Duck and cover!*
America. So well-practiced,
so ill-prepared.

un-earthed manuscript remarkably preserved except ending

in the beginning
we lived in nothing
more than caves huddling
around too much time to our next meal
and dreamed friendlier worlds

our highest art expressed in four-footed symbols
finest oratory to a purple berry or greasy nut
tribal chant to a flowing spring
war song to protect it

and the voice said look up
and the vaulted stars could be seen at midday
moving in perfect circle
like a moist finger on the rim of a chalice
filling it with aqueous songs of space
and we composed poems and knew
that they were poems and it was good

and a voice said enough of that
arrange everything into patterns
and we charted our boats
no voice said
arrange everything
and we charted our hopes

and voice said
now let hope grow and bear fruit
and hope ripened into prayer
      oh let my spear fly true

and voice said
spread subdue all thou seest
and we populated earth and heaven with ourselves
and gorged on our rituals in return for our favors

we claimed it all until earth was smothered
in our jangling audacity
and discarded rinds of industry

and voic_ _aid now_

I Don't Mean

I don't mean to doubt your faith but
      why doesn't it make you good to me?

I don't mean to question your scriptures
but why are the sweet parts applied to you
and the harsh parts to me?

I don't mean to be aloof but why does god love you
unconditionally but me conditionally?

I don't mean to sound unpatriotic
but why does the god of the universe bless
America over other nations, and before that Rome,
or France, or Germany, or Spain, then England?

I don't mean to risk your wrath but why does god
look and act like the latest rulers?

I don't mean to appear radical but why does god favor
your race over mine?

I don't mean to feel cheated, but why does god answer
your prayers and not mine – when you got the job I didn't,
and the traffic lights you believe worked for you
made me miss my friend's last moments?

I don't mean to impugn your justice but why does god love
sinners like you more than sinners like me?

I don't mean to question your motives but why does accepting
your religion put me and mine under you and yours?

I don't mean to sound bitter but why is there no room for me
in the land, the neighborhood, your family, your heart?

I don't mean to dislike your god of grace but why gift
the one truth to you and leave others in damning ignorance?

I don't mean to be impertinent but how come god welcomes
prayer in any language but only English can be spoken here?

I don't mean to be skeptical about the universality
of your religion but why do I have to amputate my culture
but you get to keep yours?

I don't mean to be in your face but why can't you see me?

I don't mean to speak so loudly but why can't you hear me?

I don't mean to doubt your faith but
        why doesn't it make you good to me?

The Poet

"In Latin America, we learn early that our lives are worth little."
Laura Yusem, director, *Paso de dos*, Buenos Aires, 1990

These are your words.
They condemn you, not I.

> *He keeps Parliaments wedged*
> *in the stained crouch*
> *of his middle finger. He also*
> *smokes profusely.*

> The following editorial…

> Now to Hector, our special correspondent.
> Hector coined the phrase "Age of Impunity"
> to summarize the times we are living in.
> Audiences should be aware: the following
> images are shocking. Hector?

> …does not represent…

> I'm standing here, live. Behind me
> ballooned figures, all of them badly burned,
> bobbing up and down the river like
> so much sewage in a gutter…

You are quite the poet.

> *He is handsome – and who*
> *dare say he's not? –*
> *with a pretty beak,*
> *that ties the truth in knots.*

...the positions...

...many with mouths agape, gargling death.
Here again we see the methods of a brutal
dictator masquerading as president of a fake
democracy based on ersatz elections,
who once said: Progress costs, damn it!
Beans or bullets! You decide!

Heaven must be with him.
Wherever he travels several
scantily clad cherubs attend him.

Yes, such a poet.
Your words should
be enshrined somewhere.
I'll see to it, personally.

...or policies...

That from the man whose prison
is nicknamed "The Arrest Home"
and political prisoners are called "Residents."
What they eat is lowered and what they
evacuate is lifted in the same bucket, and they
pass eternity in dungeons below sea level,
scrawling words with their fingernails
into walls softened by ancient slime.

...of this station.

Hector here.
   You there.
Don't care?
   Soon despair.

The Monuments Version

Stone workers clamber
across the giant heads of giant
men the rest of them still
trapped in the mountain, Lilliputians
with their tackle and tools
crisscrossing in ant trails
over each Gulliver-like face, ants
scrabbling away the hard
inedible parts, extracting only
the sweet smooth morsels
to be carried in machine-like
obedience through their runs
and tunnels and deposited in lightless
chambers where they await to be consumed
by succeeding generations of the colony.

Lazrus

Wat im talk bout to Jesus
and all dem disciple wat follow im
after Jesus raise im from de dead? Lazrus
make de best preacher-man. Cuz
Lazrus see de dead ting. im see wat comin.

Lazrus name ees from de Heebroo-man.
Dat mean – God ees my help – and God sure help im
dat day. And stir up de hornet too. Jesus
so love Lazrus dat if im wuz dere
when im sick by de devil, Jesus heal im quick
and im not make dem master so mad.
Cuz Jesus be freein people from suffrin
and death
and no ting de free man hate more dan freedom. Today

Jesus still makin de free man mad.
Cuz dey so wicked
dey rather keep dem slave
dan to listen im wat raise de dead from de toom.
Dey hard in de heart like Pharoh. But Jesus
our Moses
come to deliver de children from bondage
in Egypt-land down
down in de south. And de good book
dont say no mo bout Lazrus. But dis too hard

for de free man. So de free man say, ol Lazrus flee
de death plot by dem wicked man in de north
and come here to de south, where Paul de posle
make im de first bishop, wit em all de fancy clothe
and everyting wat his momma don give im.
But south-man Lazrus

never smile. Cuz im die and come down
down to hades
and dat no ting to smile bout. Even when im die de second time
Lazrus dont stop dere. De free man take
de bone and ting far
far to Constantee and
even to dem Russian.

But de north-man say dis a lie. Lazrus and im two sister
dey banish to sea by dem enemy of de Christian
in de south-land. But God save Lazrus and im become
de first bishop in de north-land, til im beheaded
by dem bad Roman from de south wat kill Jesus.

And dat still dont stop wit de nine live ting.
Cuz de north-man take Lazrus bone and ting
travelin too. But de south-man brag dey got
de Lazrus head
wat dey say ees better
dan de leg or de brest or de wing in de north.

And all de time
ol Lazrus,
im just laff at de free man.
But im only laff inside.
Cuz Lazrus see de dead ting.
im see wat comin.
And dat no ting to smile bout.

Rogue

160 years away, a slave
is squatting in the midnight hedgerows.
His body stinks of desperation, metal spittle
stings his mouth, heart drums so loudly
in his ears he fears the dogs will hear.

He picks his way towards an angelic voice
that cuts the moonless gloom, singing,
*Steal away, steal away, steal away
to Jesus.* He praises god to be unbound.
His master praises god when he is found,
and in order to obey the "laws of heaven"
he hangs the slave beneath a leafy haven. At this,

the earth shook, lightning spilt out of the sky
like blood from a slit artery, an ocean fell,
and towns and farms flooded, cemeteries
gave up their dead like the rapture, caskets
ruptured open, occupants missing, empty clothes
strewn as far north as the Monongahela River.
Northern papers called it a celestial event, God
bearing witness from heaven. 160 years away,

there hangs a luminous body, recently
discovered by astronomers, the first of many,
with a number but no name. It is designated
rogue because it circles no star.

Lines

                1960s

                      The lines are disappearing.
            I go 'round saying,
                    The lines are disappearing,
            and inevitably the response,
What lines?
            And I say,
                    Exactly! I rest my case.
      Then, silence.
                And that look. Like
                              it's me.

            Now, everywhere I go and
            to everything and everyone I meet,
            I say,
                    The lines are disappearing.
            And it   and   they say to me,
What lines?   Or   (and this makes me want to home run
                  heads),
Good riddance.
            Like
                I made all this up.
              Like
                  I'm the one's crazy?

                1990s

            Family can't take it anymore.
                But I keep saying,
                    The lines are disappearing, and
                        one in a hundred, eyes
                        like he won the slots,
                        chimes back,
                Damn straight. Been sayin
                same shit for years. Where you
                from brother? Buy you a drink?

2017

                    Well, y'all are fake news, but
                    I'll tell you just to tell you. That
                    thing on? Truth, we ain't never
                    been gone. We're the one's
                    been silenced – by the PC
                    police – and the fact-feds,

    like
        we're the ones rewriting history,
            like diversity
                ain't code for genocide.

                    That's why we're marching,
                    see, exercising our divine right
                    to make things right again.

Draw a great big fat streak on the ground & say, *The lines are back.*

for those who hate blm but claim they would have loved mlk   1

thing is
they are not angels

they do not dance
on the head of a pin

quadrennial

this is the time
light grows scarce
barely sifts through the interstices
of the half-closed eyelids of the dead

but this time
is like no other

this time
night is rock
to light's scissors
in a land devoid
of paper

this time
night suffocates light
under a bowl of dust

this time
night feasts
on wild endangered light
hunted and dressed
seasoned
baked in a flaky
crust and served
from hell's kitchen
by the
devil himself

for those who hate blm but claim they would have loved mlk   2

they are too busy dancing on our heads
and when we play our music they sit down

El Paso and Dayton

Ain't brave. Just know he couldn't
have gotten one past the scanners.
How the bird managed to get past
the doors and passageways,
throngs of people and the security area
I don't know. But I know
it will be dead soon. Can you imagine
the flak if everyone had to stop
so we could save this little bird?

Earlier that day it landed suddenly
on the floor in the middle of people bustling
their baggage and cell phone kids,
to destinies and deals pending. By now

we've all heard. Nine at one, twenty-three at the other
will be the final tally. I buy a biscuit
at a breakfast joint in the restaurant row
near my gate so I can feed it to the bird. The cashier
thinks it's for me. *Jus a plain biscuit? No gravy? You sure?*
You don't even want some jelly, honey? No nothin? Somehow

my plan sounds farcical in a southern drawl so severe
that the left side of her lips dips and returns
after each sentence like an old typewriter.

I pay the ludicrous price of $3.95 for the small biscuit,
walk over to the bird and throw it crumbs
before boarding. A meaty man,
skin the color of ash and a sneer like lust,
says, "Dude, what's the point?" I feel lucky
to be in one of those few spaces, so I respond,
"Dude, it's better than thoughts and prayers."

for those who hate blm but claim they would have loved mlk   3

we pin them to our lapels and chain

them round our wrists like charms but

they fly

off the chains of our domesticated piety

and spurn the flatulent love
we love to give the prophets
but only from the safety of

              historical distance

Prayer for Nothing

No fusillade of jackhammers laying cover
for invading troops of buildings and streets
walled off to all collateral damage. No
politicians like barkers at a carnival
passing out buttons and balloons
and tickets to grotesque things you can't turn
your eyes from. No flying monkeys
expelling out of every conspiratorial talk show
orifice. No faith the size of a bullet.
I could go on, Lord, but at this point
I'd be happy if nothing happened today.

3. VATOS

Vatos

> Vatos are made not born

Homeboy's family were full-blooded Tarahumara Indians who came to Los Angeles from the Sierra Madre Occidental in northern Mexico. His people (I read once in *National Geographic*) are legendary long-distance runners known for beating American ultramarathoners while wearing sandals and stopping occasionally for a smoke. Unconquered by the Spanish and centuries of colonialism, it took the invasion of foreign capitalists and tourists to finally erode one of the most intact Indian cultures in the Western hemisphere. "Foreigners," he used to say, "drove me from my home to the US of A's where I am treated like a foreigner."

> Americans, they love freedom but not for brown people. They love him who had "no place to lay his head" but not poor people. And they sure love Indians – that defeat rival football teams, and win baseball pennants, or faithfully assist a masked, Clorox-clean avenger of justice of a yesteryear that never was, but they do not love Indians. America, the Houdini of republics.

Cops in our barrios gave us not one quark or lepton of respect. When we were thirteen years old, Homeboy and I were walking home from the movies one evening when suddenly two cops grabbed us from behind and began barking into our waxen faces, ordering us to "pick it up." "Pick what up?" I asked, and thereupon received a savage blow to my jaw. That day I learned that a sufficient blow to the face really does make you see stars like Wile E. Coyote. Except whereas Wile E. has a healing factor more dope than Deadpool, I ended up with TMJ for twenty years. (To this day, my jaw's slight misalignment causes me to bite the inside of my mouth when I eat.)

A thunderous bang in my ears, and adrenalin, I think, caused me to snap to and my legs were possessed with the speed force. We ran as fast as we could. When I looked back I realized that the cops were not following. The hell? Homeboy was behind me, built for distance not speed. His nose and lips were bleeding, his singlet bright with blood. Something in his aspect frightened me. As he got closer I saw that his right arm was so shattered it dangled hideously like a string of sausages.

Everything that had shut down for flight mode now discharged like a fire hose. I wept asthmatically, from shock at how arbitrary survival on earth can be, from horror at how fragile the human body is, from disgust at how perfectly evil people can be, from anger at the feckless god who let it happen, from shame because Homeboy was in pieces and didn't shed a tear.

Homeboy's family was poor and that put hospital and proper surgery out of the picture. In those days one might turn to someone's family friend who stocked grocery shelves or laid roofing shingle during the week, and on evenings and weekends did anything from exorcisms to dentistry – pulling out demons of drink and infidelity y poca vergüenza[1], or pulling rotting teeth from the jaws of poor people with needle-nose pliers sterilized in rum. So some bargain basement modern Prometheus just bandaged Homeboy's arm together. After it healed, if you could call it that, girls retreated at the sight of him, like frightened villagers before Frankenstein's nameless creature. The injury left him with a cadaverous aggregation that he could rotate a full 360, at the end of it his hand with the middle finger at attention for anyone who made fun of his mutant abilities, a special up yours – with a twist. That fateful confrontation changed forever how Homeboy looked, feral, like he'd been abandoned as an infant at the gate of Chino State Prison. That day we began to discard childhood.

We were vatos locos.[2] Kids who couldn't hurt the man, but we could hurt our own. Kids who hurled verbal chingasos[3] at each

---

[1] Poca vergüenza = lack of humility or honor (mild); little or no shame (strong).
[2] Vato is Spanish slang for gang member, tough guy, or just dude. Vatos locos loosely translates to fearless or crazy dudes.
[3] Chingaso = a hit, blow or bump, deliberate or by accident. A chingaso can also mean being screwed over, cheated or oppressed by some person, group, party or government. Often laced with sexual profanity as in "go screw yourself."

other, who behaved like a herd of horny elk stamping, champing and locking antlers for the prize does in the wood. Kids who struggled for dominance, recognition, respect, or at least relief from a ritual ass-kicking. Kids enthralled, like bugs to a zapper, to the cruel do-as-I-say-but-not-as-I-do dictators. Little more than shit to these lords of the flies, we nevertheless kowtowed and followed them, with tragic consequences.

Nightmare of teachers, we left huge nut-threaded bolts instead of apples on their desks, talked out of turn incessantly, ditched school fearlessly, turned classrooms into boxing arenas, lit desks on fire, made teachers quit. Every kid in school wants to be valued, wants recognition. We just went about getting it differently than the legendary jocks, valedictorians and other alumni whose names and images still adorn the official plaques at the school. We made our own placas[4] – spraying, squiggling and slashing our tags on every natural and man-made object along the entire chain of being.

We were just kids, but we had crossed the Rubicon of vato-ness. Young vatos cross many such rivers of no return, the last one being, all too soon, the Styx.

We smoked because real vatos are men, popular, direct-talking, girl-attracting men who always had a clever line to a challenge, or a clenched fist, even if you're only thirteen or fourteen and don't have enough hair under your jeans to impress a peach. That was the propaganda in the era of the unambivalent American smoker on TV and film, magazines and billboards. And we inhaled it all.[5]

The delusion foisted on las rucas[6], and all women, was arguably worse. In the early 20th century tobacco executives discovered how Freudian psychology could be used to get women to link smoking in public to the feminist movement and thereby increase the population of smokers. An elaborate scheme was staged in 1929 during the annual Easter Parade in New York City. The

---

[4] Placa = more literally, a license plate, (award) plaque. Slang = personal or gang name, tag or symbol.
[5] This paragraph is adapted from my poem, "How to quit smoking," found in this collection.
[6] Ruca = Mexican slang for girlfriend of a Chicano gang member, any girlfriend or "old lady."

press had been tipped off and were lying in wait for the scoop. At a signal, several paid women scandalously lit their cigarettes, took a hit, raised them to the sky like so many statues of liberty and shouted the carefully prepared slogan, "torches of freedom." A social taboo imposed by men was now shattered by men who gave to women their own Freudian phalluses, which they now brazenly held in their mouths in public. What could be more emancipated than that? By the 1960s, the sexual revolution was a juggernaut and cigarette commercials were pitching a new slogan to women, "You've come a long way, baby!" So cigarette companies gave boys their manhood, girls their freedom, and both cancer. In return we made them rich. Tobacco execs, what balls, what impossible balls.

There was similar propaganda to alcohol. We drank beer, wine and hard liquor like Tang until a fight broke out – which happened with the regularity of a natural law – or until we threw up a booze smoothie mixed with corn nuts, Chunky bars and Swizzle Sticks in someone's parent-absent home and woke up in the park with no memory and a body weak as a death rattle. Then some primal thing still left in our brainstem made us rasp and shamble our way home, tranquil hamlet in the dim moonlight about to experience the horror of their children-turned-zombies to all vergüenza, shame.

Only a few of us smoked pot back then, and even so just occasionally. One joint could cost more than a pack of cigarettes. Grifa[7] was simply too expensive for kids who never got an allowance from parents who couldn't imagine what children needed money for (or maybe because they could imagine).

We sniffed glue, the cheapest brain-blasting high available to poor kids. And you didn't need a fake I.D. or secret code under cover of night to get it. You could buy rubber cement or model glue along with your Bazooka gum and Orange Crush in almost any store. Glue-trips made time freeze, swallowed whole swaths of time. Once I was watching some guys on a field playing catch football and – as frequently happens with glue-sniffing where one moment everything's as ordinary as 1950's television and the next you're in the Phantom Zone – every human hardened where they

---

[7] Grifa = slang, marijuana.

stood like action figures, the football suspended in the air. I too was petrified, by fear that I might finally have committed the unpardonable sin, condemned to remain forever trapped in that grotesque still life. Then, as suddenly as it came, the high ended and I found myself in another location entirely, laughing at something someone said, though I can't remember what to this day, much of the memory murdered along with the brain cells that had borne it.

True time loss. Fox Mulder would have soiled himself. Somewhere in the dim recesses of my public school education I recall some teacher expounding that time is not absolute. Big deal. Every glue-sniffing vato who ever flunked woodshop knew that. Glue-sniffing, one of those self-destructive activities we knew was self-destructive. There was this one old esse[8] that everybody called "The Walker," because he would walk the streets sniffing a bag laced with glue, dressed in baggy pants, singlet, suspenders, hush puppies, bandana, and impunity. Vato could barely string five words together. Blew his mind completely, and we knew it. Made fun of it. But by then we had grown huevos de piedra[9] that had liberated us from the banality of common sense.

We were vatos locos. We who attracted after-school crowds to regular gladiatorial bouts and never once held a compassionate thumbs up nor mourned those who lay in the dust not for the honor of the gods, not because it is sweet and right to die for your country, not because it is better to die on one's feet than to live on one's knees, but for a mere misstep at the water fountain.

We were vatos locos. We who walked with arms swinging not along our sides but away from our bodies, one human demanding two spaces – in a land that told us, "Stay on your side of the line." Our torsos coolly recumbent so that to see ahead our eyes had to look down, down on the world that looked down on us. Our walk and dress said, we're unique. Our jargon said, we keep secrets, yeah, from you, pendejo![10] Our aspect said, get out of our way. Our families could not compete with this family. We

---

[8] Esse = slang for dude, bro, gang member.
[9] Huevos de piedra = literally, eggs of stone; slang for testicles of stone, or fearless.
[10] Pendejo = idiot, moron.

católicos in name only. We who were invisible in the public school curriculum. We whom the upper classes treated like the plague, and white politicians (was there any other kind?) spoke of like a priest speaks of original sin. We whom employers cheated and the media presented as a problem. We from neighborhoods that cops did not protect and serve but policed. We who had only Tonto as a TV character who looked like us, though we were always suspicious why his name in Spanish meant Dummy. We who became supremely indifferent to gringos and negritos[11], republicans and democrats, capitalists and communists, spaces races and nuclear standoffs.

We were vatos locos, and this was our world. Not the one we made or chose to be born in, but the one we hacked off the hegemonic pie, the one that must take no small part of the blame for what we were.

Prequel

In the summer of 1969, just about the time the Apollo 11 astronauts were headed for the moon and the history books, a middle school ganglet called The Dark Knights headed for a decrepit theater that was trying to stay in operation by showing double features and charging only 50¢ (last desperate act of bygone rococo and art deco theaters doomed by their single screens). We had some time before the first show, so we hung out at a bowling alley, listened to piped-in music and feasted on Winchell's donuts and chocolate milk. (Despite everything I've said, I sometimes forget that in key respects we were still kids, and if it were a choice between cigarettes and beer or donuts and chocolate milk, most of us would have picked the latter by default.)

We ate and listened to Archie Bell and the Drells' "Tighten Up," followed by "Ooo Baby Baby," by Smokey Robinson and the

---

[11] Gringos = white North Americans, derogatory or not. Negritos = black persons. Growing up I remember "negrito" or "negrita" (feminine) as a term of endearment, as it is common for Puerto Ricans to date and marry across color lines, as did my white mother and brown father, then black step-father. In the racialized U.S., the English equivalent was often an insult. The Spanish "mayate" was used for maximum racial insult against black people.

Miracles. It was as if bowling alley management had a system that played music according to the tastes of the tribe that happened to be there at the time. Güeros?[12] "Your Cheatin' Heart." Vatos? "Crystal Blue Persuasion," and so on. Smart. They knew to soothe the savage beasts. But they slipped with the next song, The Fifth Dimension's "Aquarius, Let the Sunshine In," my second favorite song of the year, and my secret.

> Harmony and understanding
> Sympathy and trust abounding
> No more falsehoods or derisions
> Golden living dreams of visions
> Mystic crystal revelation
> And the mind's true liberation
> Aquarius! Aquarius!

No, I don't recall the vatos holding hands across the barrio and singing in unison to that. I had to be careful not to let my head bob or finger tap to the beat. I may as well hop on a table and wiggle my ass to "Simon Says" by the 1910 Fruitgum Company, paragon of Bubblegum pop, the worst music that ever shat into the human ear. My rep would have been mierda.[13] We began to leave and before Aquarius was finished another song started: Harry Nilsson's "Everybody's Talkin'." The vatos really despised that one, reacted with verbal violence when the yodeling started. I loved this song. I kept that to myself too.

After all the animus to gringo music (we were required to hate it, you see), we went to the cinema and what did the vatos pay to watch, a Western called "The Wild Bunch," and loved it. When it finished nobody but Homeboy wanted to watch the second feature. Going to the movies was a special treat, so I stayed too. The rest of the vatos split. We'd meet up with them later at the bowling alley and then walk home together. The second feature was a British drama called "The Prime of Miss Jean Brodie," a film I had never heard of. While we were waiting for it to start, Homeboy talked about how a then vernal Maggie Smith deserved the best actress Academy Award (which she would in fact win the

---

[12] Güeros = lighter skinned persons of any ethnic group, derogatory or not.
[13] Mierda = crap.

following year). He went on about the film's differences from the Muriel Spark novel, and the climactic "assassin" scene at the end, a scene he told me to look out for, all of which meant he'd seen the movie more than once. I fully expected the "assassin" scene to include a sniper and some doomed government whistleblower, but it ended up being about relational betrayal.

Homeboy was simply not the same vato as his public persona. Don't know why he risked opening up to me this way. Maybe because staying to watch the second movie said something about me. Homeboy didn't even use our slang, and I found myself not using it either. I could have been talking to a film critic, a playwright or a novelist. I never saw this side of him. He hid it, this love of art, this intimacy with literature, this enlightened soul. I hid things too. I never told any friend that I used to walk to the local library regularly and check out books to read, from a popular translation of Homer's *Iliad* and *Odyssey* to Fred Gipson's *Old Yeller*, and I certainly would never have admitted that I knew all the lyrics to "Everybody's Talkin'" and practiced repeatedly and failed to match Nilsson's yodeling.

After the movie we began the long walk home. From talk about the movie we moved on to books we liked. Scott's *Ivanhoe*. Did people once really speak like poets? Even the insults were marvelous. We discussed how Frank Baum's *The Wizard of Oz* was better than the movie, and that was saying something. It showed how belief in ourselves flourishes when others believe in us. That dealing with evil doesn't have to mean responding in kind. That courage is not the absence of fear but the conviction that there are things greater than fear. This was shit no vato ever talked about. Hypocrisy is terrible, but it is most terrible when you have no one to be honest with.

I felt at last that I had found someone who like me saw through all the bullshit of peer hegemony, our mercurial omerta, the ineffectual violence, and we wondered why we submitted to it all. We wondered if there were more vatos like us who thought that our rebelliousness was a road to nowhere, however we justified it as a righteous loogie hocked into the hamburger order of white America. That if we admitted who we really were to the other vatos they would likely betray us. Assassins. So why did we consider them our friends? We wondered if we dared to do what it took to be free from captivity to what would surely turn out to be insignificant sub-cultural moments in the larger tapestry of American history. Do something large with our lives. Anger, arrogance, vengeance, violence are not large but small, small because most of the time their expressions are random and selfish, serve no noble purpose, and cause more casualties in our own homes and barrios than victories against enemies. But then do what? If to be innocent, pure, and fit for heaven with King of Kings Tab Hunter one had to be white as snow, how many allies of poor brown people could there be in the universe?

We had no answers. But we decided then and there to find a way out. Absorbed in talk, we lost track of time and lagged well behind the rest of our set. Suddenly, ahead of us in the alley behind a row of homes off the main drag, there was a loud disruption, like overturned trash cans and the general sounds of mayhem accompanied by the diabolical laughter of our absconding friends, whom we assumed had visited some expression of humiliation on a poor bag lady in her cardboard condo, or some decrepit viejo[14] in his backyard guzzling Thunderbird and getting even with god.

After a while we decided to catch up with them when suddenly two cops grabbed us from behind and began barking into our waxen faces...

---

[14] Viejo = old man.

4. SEASONAL AFFECTIVE DISORDER

Seasonal Affective Disorder

My eyes are butterflies
in the waning summer's days,
pale-winged imago foraging
for the Goldilocks zone
in the deep dark cosmic woods.
Give me the conspiracy of stars.
Give me crate loads of moments,
however unrequited,
dreamers' dreams heaped
in the attics and closets
of the world. Give me
all of life's unused lotto tickets,
now the sum of past's perfections.
I stand here waiting
at winter's door.

Special Relativity

A friend's father has passed and
I've no time to comfort her so
my fingers shred the keyboard like
a blues guitarist's belated regrets before
continuing my way through the infinity mirror
of next multitasking through the city
swarm surrounded by gleaming ziggurats with
their inner mysteries and those incomprehensible
beings we placate not to fail who gaze all-
knowing down canyons of concrete and glass that
echo the squelch and hum of human machinery echo
glittering sirens racing over mumbling
streets on this world racing through the feral
dark at 108000 kmh so I have pulled over to
let it rocket past and
my attention has perched on a window
display for standing amid the ascetic winter scape is
a manikin dressed in summer
wear in mute rebuke of the words Scripture *Let
tomorrow's concerns concern themselves* sunhat
attached to one hand rests in a caress
along an adipose free thigh and the other gestures
in the direction the face is facing serene as marble
insensible to our-place-in-the-chain or the wait of hope
but the sirens fade, clocks resume. And
I am re-merged with the brimming world.

Where is Everybody?

> Skeptical of theories that the cosmos should contain a high yield
> of intelligent life, Enrico Fermi asked, "Where is everybody?"

I read somewhere that a poet
is one who looks out the window
and sees worlds teeming with life.
Today I looked out the window
and felt like Fermi.
Where is everybody?
Science does not believe
in angels. It has never doubted
aliens. But with each
new technology the universe got bigger,
distances so preposterous
that if we're not alone
we may as well be. It was all
smaller once and we were bigger,
Earth not yet a pale blue dot,
fragile lifeboat on a sea of ink.
Small as it was
the universe was overpopulated,
mostly with star-mapped beasts,
yo-yo divinities and outright
monsters it's true, but at least
Earth was Grand Central Station.

How to quit smoking

It's important to get you early, no later
than middle school, when you're as likely
to resist conformity as a sardine.

Trotting among a pack of mutts following
a pure-bred alpha to the 7-Eleven, you watch
him buy two packs of cigarettes, his lieutenants
each buy one, and you in the queue, like some cult
member obliged to renounce your brains
and wait for the second coming at the corner
of Wilshire and Fairfax on the Miracle Mile. Why

do you do this to yourself? Because
smoking is what men do – real, popular,
direct-talking, female-attracting men
who always have a clever line to a challenge
or a clenched fist –
even if you're only twelve or thirteen
and don't have enough hair under your jeans
to impress a peach. That was the propaganda
in the era of the unambivalent American smoker
on TV and film, magazines and billboards.
And you inhaled it all.

The cashier looks down at you
like something vile lodged in his Vibram-soled
shoes, asks gruffly what you want,
and with panic you choose the brand you hope
tells everyone everything they need to know
about you. Then the reprobate illegally sells
a pack of Kool menthol cigarettes to the boy
with a popsicle voice and a face erupting

with puberty. You know nothing about Kools.
Perhaps you heard they were the favorite
of Nat King Cole, who chain-smoked them claiming
they mellowed his famous voice (but silenced it
when he died of lung cancer in 1965). No. You buy

them purely for the association of the name.

Then you take your first drags. First time smokers
are always good for a laugh. You're expected
to get past convulsing and accept
the toxic fog, like clueless 1950s children running
alongside DDT trucks cheering the clouds. It helps, then,

if you're thirteen years old and you connect smoking
with that alpha, who will become a man's man,
almost the twin of that famous billboard cowboy
who managed to tame the wild frontier, build cabins,
ranches, and towns, drive herds and bring home
the fat of others' lands, carve up mountains, guzzle rivers,
and still look minty fresh when he lights up
on the hand-hewn porch at night, feet propped on railing,
moon shining benevolently on his brow. But years later,

cancer has shriveled him to a third of his normal mass,
and from his bed, bent like a fetus,
he'd speak the words if he could.

American Sentences

The evidence includes mental and
        physical abnormalities.

A saying goes that they're only renting space
        in someone else's head.

The accused are all women, young and old,
        thousands fleeing to safety.

Some are said to have retractable claws
        that shred men to gelatin.

Some knew that their husbands were with other women,
        caught them in the act.

How could they have done that, say prosecutors,
        if they were not witches?

Blur, blend, brew, flich, flood, flew,
        million-mile pedantic panic all for being you.

They're accused of generating force-fields
        that disintegrate man-words.

Even though male energy can neither be
        created nor destroyed.

The unpardonable sin
        is their appalling lack of gratitude.

Oh, and this is always happening
in some other part of the world.

The Bad News

> "...My rifle is my best friend. It is my life...I must fire my rifle true. I must shoot straighter than my enemy who is trying to kill me...."
> - Attributed to Major General William H. Rupertus, USMC, 1942

We denominate you as object target, enemy, not us, other. We study you, everything, anything, even rifle through trash for all useful information. We work from fortified positions and catalog your relative strengths and exploitable weaknesses. Our recon knows no equal. Scholars from our most hallowed halls of learning have done their jobs so we can do ours. Our revered leaders have shepherded us to this point. All is in readiness. We take aim out our windows from cover at the back of the room, from our grassy knolls, or point blank from your trusted side. We maneuvered you to the kill box. Our satellite recon is god and god sees all, can number the hairs on your head, sends live feeds to the confab, which relays intel to the assets. We track precise wind velocity and direction, even account for the Coriolis force of the earth's rotation, fine tune trajectories, lase targets. Mission assets are disciplined as monks, vowed to absolute obedience, to accept that a thing is white even if we see black, vowed to silence. Then, the word is given. We shoot. Here comes the bad news. The round hits with the force of a thunderbolt, taking you apart, everything you were and are and hoped to be. There's not the least thing clinical about it. We shoot you with the truth. And the only thing we feel is the recoil of the rifle.

Who Sinned?
(Por Ernesto, papá y obreo)

"Letter to The Sacred Congregation for the Propagation of the Faith"
- Mirahijo Del Río, El Hereje, *Journals and Letters*, Vol. 2, pp. 32-33.
Translated from the Spanish.

> *As he went along, he saw a beggar blind from birth. His disciples asked him, 'Rabbi, who sinned, this man or his parents, that he was born blind?'* - Gospel According to John 9:1-3

In accounts of his life the infancy and childhood narratives are missing, as if his was a nativity without parents or country or history of any kind worthy of remembrance, but like Athena, sprang forth inexplicably, fully adult and fully armed, not for war but work, and here we enter into the singularly despotic feature of his life – if such can be called – work, for he was conscripted to grow the cane, our laws disqualifying him from doing little else, and so he worked, worked as few of us have ever worked, and as he worked so he prayed to old divinities with new names for proper parts sun and rain, and months later laid his machete to the stem of the mature plants, being careful not to injure the roots and incur the wrath of the island's new supreme god, whom he knew to be fickle, fickle about whom he fancied so that he dare not risk displease him more, and he tied the cane into bundles and carried them on his back for the rum-makers, and the rest of the time carried baskets on his head with little meals to sell in the villages, and at day's end returned home – if all went well – with a few coins, a few bruises and the stink of rum, and in this course has persisted his whole life, his body now broken, his wife by the pox taken, the welfare and whereabouts of his children unknown, and as he can work no more he begs daily at the cross-roads of the grand avenue leading to the city, depending on the costive charity of the children of light who now rule this island, and whom he is ever obliged to bless. So, tell me, Fathers, who sinned that this man was born black?

College Diner
(for G. W.)

A trickle that soon swells. Lines for
forks and spoons, eggs and bacon,
oatmeal, oj, coffee, careers, proposals.

A boyish man, thin as a chalk line, head
pummeled with cowlicks, feeding
spoonfuls of cereal to the book in front of his face.

A woman, skin the color of treacle,
piping music into her ears,
thumb wrestling a phone, feeding note cards
into her head, and food into her mouth,
no action seems more important than the other.

An elfish woman, still in pajamas,
hair like late autumn, picks
dispassionately at a plate of shadows,
stares intensely at the same page
waiting for the revelation she hopes
lies beyond the physical text.

A chiseled lad, still steaming
from the gym, carries his tray of nutrition
like an offering to an altar.

A professor, age now in sync with the history
he teaches, ponders the future,
takes notes for a poem.

The Plunge

The other day I saw one of those internet videos that go viral. It was
another collection of falls and epic fails where the skateboarder
slides down a stairway rail, slips, straddles and scrambles his
eggs, or the toasted rotund mother-in-law at a wedding who
kicks up her heels one degree too many and falls backward
spread-eagle revealing that which must not be named, or
the stereotypical jello-y bikinied thing who on a dare
plunges into the drink far below and emerges bare
breasted, eyes like a squirrel in headlights, or
the mook who snaps a cigarette lighter to his
butt and the ensuing explosion sends
him running from a conflagration of
laughter. And that wiry lad one cold
December day at a backyard pool
surrounded by friends daring him
to jump into the freezing water,
polar bear plunge they call it.
He runs, leaps high in the air,
body in a cannon ball for
maximum entry effect – at
that moment no one in the
world was more free – and
lands square on his coccyx
on the crust of ice which,
to his excruciating
surprise, does not, I repeat,
does not yield, and which
may as well have been a dive
onto concrete. And isn't
that like life much of
the time? Not the falls
and fails, not the crying
while others laugh, but
that we foolishly,
gloriously
keep
plung-
ing
in.

The Gospel of Bulldog

Bulldog puppies, a roly-poly mass
of caged contestants in tag-team competition,
flapping jowls flashing rice teeth biting,
biting parts unmentionable, paws over-inflated,
skin melting on their bodies, and faces
that look like they chased a car that stopped.

"We can't hold them for another two days,"
someone says. *(Like holding them now
would subtract their intrinsic fields
and turn them into goo?)* A bald man

with the bulk of a professional wrestler,
his face so pressed to the cage, looks
like one of the litter. He can't stop talking
about them. "They have the sweetest disposition –
friendly – great with kids – they don't
get that big – absolutely lovable – love
to socialize – part of the family." He preaches

on and on, the Gospel of Bulldog,
his pregnant wife looking on with a
hallelujah face. I feel compelled to respond
to this call and accept a Bulldog puppy
into my heart. I want, no, I need one of those
so-ugly-they're-cute little bastards. Then

I see an odd number fixed inconspicuously
on the right bottom corner of the cage: $3000.00.
$3000.00. Another evangelist asking for money.

Pulp Fiction Women

Here's to the pulp fiction women. By men you were made
for men's dreams. How could they deny you their dimes?
Let the horror and hilarity begin.

To the virtuous pulp fiction women, of the whitest white –
with no variableness nor shadow of turning in you – unlike
we who were always the villains.

To the beautiful pulp women, under fine threads or tatters
your bosoms always unholstered and ready for a shootout,
bellies perfect as snowflakes, your eyes, bullwhips,
all your curves and tangents bound in a Western declination,
even if you were from Venus or Alpha C.

Here's to you, you poor dumbed pulp women, who always went
toward bumps in the night and other nexus-scary shit, instead
of the hell away; who always managed to trip and let
snail-paced monsters catch you, and rarely thought
to wear anything more than bubble helmets and bikinis
in the meat lockers and fry vats of space.

To the good-girl-in-bondage pulp women, needing rescuing
by males from males of every imaginable form – humanoid,
robotic, demonic, bestial, microbial – that stalked you,
stole you, bound you, gagged you, drugged you, unzipped
every atom of you, exsanguinated you, gutted you, beat you,
strangled you, stabbed you, shot you, lased you, chopped you,
minced you, mashed you, baked you, boiled you, broiled you,
served you with croutons, chewed you, swallowed you,
and savored every last quark and lepton of you.

Here's to you, contrapasso pulp women, witches and demonesses,
high priestesses and high-heeled amazons and queens of space,
who composed your own justice like poets, and lured men
to your dens, your chambers and altars and all-women empires,
who flew down on broomsticks and flicked your pig-morphing
curses, who toyed with the lizards in men's brains, and held them
in bondage in penal colonies, and clicked your alien nobs

and fried them to shriveled sticks.

Here's to you, star-nursery pulp fiction women, corona-wearing mother of us all, oh, mysterious dark matter women, holding every thing together that muscular gravity alone cannot, irresistible dark energy women, undisputed masters of the universe, have mercy, now, and at the hour of our entropy.

Final Frontier

This space feels alien, complete
with a persistent droning that sounds
eerily like the score to *Forbidden Planet*.

In the space of two hours I have been probed
and examined by no less than seven
people, each one insinuating their role by first
scanning one of my bracelets and asking me

to verify the same personal information,
in the event that I was abducted
and replaced with a doppelganger
whose baffling case has turned into an X-File.

I am made to sit recumbent on a thing
I hear repeatedly called a bed, but this
is pure casuistry meant to calm me down,

for it is obvious to any objective observer
that it is a flight chair for space travel,
as one may confirm from

the restraints, computers, lighted panels, life support
monitors and an octopus of tubes
and wires labeled 'Oxygen' and 'Vacuum' and

'Press in Case of Emergency'. Have you ever noticed
how a hospital room is conveniently designed
for our journey to the final frontier?

If obituaries told all

He was a husband who used to say, *Behind
every great man is a good woman*, behind
being the operative word.

He was into the life of the spirit,
if you count Thunderbird and Ripple,
and Brew 101.

He was a big salesman, drove a different car
every week, none of them his.

He was a staunch believer in the institution
of marriage – told his third wife it was his two exes
that didn't.

He was a father who believed children
should take responsibility as early
as possible. *Look at wildebeest calves.* No shit,
he said, *Look at wildebeest calves.*

He got religion and became a pastor. Used to tell
his flock, *You're only young once but you can be immature
forever.* Several joked he meant this as an altar call.

He was eighty-eight. Alone. He could have been
a thousand. Point is, clarity may not come in the end.

5. HEAVEN IS OTHER PEOPLE

Of Faith and Things Seen

Sitting reading poetry one evening
in our rented cinder block bungalow
overlooking the circuit-board city

of Los Angeles, I saw a large glass-skinned spider
skittering along the baseboard and I thought,
"There is the king of house insects." Suddenly,

a fiend that looked like a scorpion but
was not a scorpion flashed from under my chair,
the one I was sitting on reading poetry,

and stomped at the spider, mangled it
in its claws and ate it with speed
and savagery to rival any acid-veined xenomorph

lurking in the vaults of Hollywood horror,
and I remember being mad at you.
I was sitting in a warm grassy courtyard

by the university chapel reading
a spiritual devotional. Ten feet from me
was a nut-brown sparrow jerking its head

side to side listening meticulously for worms
underneath its twiggy legs, and I was more enraptured
by this little creature than the words in my devotional.

In this Saint Francis mood, materializing ex-nihilo
from another dimension, a large crow flashed across
my field of vision, upon the sparrow, beaked it to death

like an old vendetta, and carried off the carcass
to dine in Darwinian splendor, and
I remember being mad at you.

Another time, feeling deeply Francis,
I was gardening and I stopped to watch

a small sorority of house wrens fluttering playfully

in and out of the bittersweet, when
a bark-colored hawk lacerated down
from a neighboring pine and snatched one mid-air

in its talons, then gone as quickly as it came.
The other wrens scattered in panic. One flew
into my chest and I cupped it in my hands. Our eyes met

and it knew that it was safe and we were best mates,
while all that remained of its friend was a flittering of wispy down
settling to the ground, and I remember being mad at you.

One morning driving to university where I taught history
that was growing uncomfortably in sync with my age,
I was on a road heading into the most beautiful dawn

I think I have ever seen: a blood-orange horizon interlaced
with crème caramel clouds like tiramisu in a crystal bowl,
in the middle, a single ray of misty light shooting upward,

as if earth was the source that illuminated heaven,
not the other way around. And underneath
all that glory, somewhere, a meal of sparrow fricassee,

a side order of spider hors d'oeuvres, at Darwin's Diner,
on this flawless dawn, god's people somewhere oppressing
god's other people, and god's people elsewhere

packing food and water and medical aid
to send to their refugee camps, and I understood
the word "awesome" in the ancient sense.

Shalom

On the horizon, clouds
pile like chalk cliffs, earth awakens

with russet skin
in the tangerine light, birds

in attendance
like cherubs. Sky and sea,

newborn twins in a looking glass, sun
waving greeting

east to west. I must be something else,
a wolf maybe, or a hawk.

I have never taken in this much.
The whole brown bosom of earth

swells with milk for a birthing.
Molecules sing in everything,

in the crackling bark of the elm
that yawns in the morning sun,

the hornbeam and mountain ash,
in the water mint that sweetens

the yodeling stream you can only
step in once.

Anniversarium[31]

from the ending of
a super massive star
from which everything
in the world is said to come
from extortionate californium
to bargain basement graphite and clay
pressed and wrapped
in the common cellulose wand
I hold in my carbon-based hand
with that amazing opposable thumb

all coalesce here
as I write to you
these words
one in particular
love
its origins elude me
that it should emerge
from the cosmic blast
completely eludes me

That time of year

Pricey and advertised with a profane
swagger, *For the one who has everything*.
A real bargain *For every occasion*,
like we don't mind being lied to. Accepted

with a diplomatic smile
then promptly disappeared
like a political dissident,
or released from its cell
and taken to the lines
of those impatiently awaiting
a prisoner exchange.

Now tables are piled with the closeouts
and BOGOs and soon to be landfill. Even the most
popular and expensive have a short shelf life,
Best Used By programmed into them,
1.0 gifts in a 2.0 world. And then

there's that cheap plastic doll
from your mother who had nothing
else to give you, now carefully preserved
in state in a glass cabinet, like a reliquary
holding saintly remains, or the necktie
your old flame gave you that you remove
from its sealed bag to get your regular hit
of her, or the child's crude clay
handprint on the mantle, and today,
if your whole world was threatened with fire,
the one thing you'd carry with you
like your own skin.

When I was a Child

When I was a child I thought a long while
what I most wanted to be.
So I made a long cape
that I put on with tape
and I jumped from a chair
to fly in the air,
but I fell down and injured my knee.

I started to cry and I asked my mom why
I could not do superman stuff.
But she taped up my knee
and said listen to me,
you're my boy and that's super enough.

When I was a child I thought a long while
that I'd try to reach up to a star.
So I made a space suit,
cardboard helmet and boots
and I ran up the stairs
as they're higher than chairs,
but I just couldn't get very far.

I started to cry and I asked my mom why
I could not reach a star.
But she just held my hand
and said, please understand,
you're my boy and a bright star you are.

When I was child I thought a long while
I'd hunt and find riches to spare.
So I went to the yard
and I dug very hard,
very hard all day long
'til my arms were long gone,
but no treasure was found anywhere.

I started to cry and I asked my mom why
I could not find treasure trove.
But she held me near
whispered in my ear,
you're my boy and I treasure your love.

When I was a child I thought a long while
after something went wrong inside me.
So I did all I could
to be good like I should
and I prayed all day long
that my illness was gone,
but I guess it was not meant to be.

I heard my mom cry and I understood why,
for my mom used to pray just like me.
And I said as I died
to my mom at my side,
I'm your boy and I always will be.

Isolde

When they look at you – hands cadaverous
And wormy, your coin-purse breasts and

Vulture's stoop, your face a dripping candle –
They do not think, there is the face that launched

A thousand ships; there is Queen Nefertiti
Who competed with religion in Egypt.

They do not think, there is Guinevere,
For whose love Lancelot broke troth with king,

Or Juliet, whose name is a synonym for love.
What are you to them but a crumpled paper

Of a woman holding up the line while counting change
With ancient eyes translucent and frail as guppies;

Patient on a weekly allowance of a few slices of bacon
With her meaningless gruel; somebody's great grand

Someone on a park bench. But it's there,
In the rusting engine of bones, on the loosening

Strings of voice, and the hollowing sockets,
Like bowls with their scoop of eyes, love's flame still

Smoldering since the day you drank the philter,
And the two of you was all there was.

But your Tristan is long dead. And now
You too. Set free from the agony of day,

Your feathery ash evidence that I did not imagine
The whole thing, that you were not a ghost

floating at the corner of my eye,
Vitreous debris burned on my retina,

Candle in my window from which I glimpsed
The ecstasy of the world of night.

Dawning

        Just dawn
soft as wren's feathers
and lithe as a dragonfly,
attired in lace of spider web
and dew-beads.

In the candelabra
of the honey locust
dappled by leaves,
a darting form
with keen obsidian eyes,
and the rowdy chromatic
songs of spring.

How generous it all is.
The frosted moon is free
to look upon. The mist
that trails the ground
like a wedding gown,
the light that wreaths
the sparkling stream
are not improved by
our *likes*, or consumer con-
fidence.

        Pause
the long, incessant sentence of your life,
put in line breaks

and stanzas that
surprise again, scan
the stresses of each line,
adjust the meter, or free
your verse altogether, repent

harsh gutturals, choose
softer syllables. This
is your turn.

Heaven is Other People

There will be no tribes or nations, only people
from every tribe and nation.
This will be hard.

There will be cultures but no captivity, differences
but no bigotry, resources but no rivalry,
feasts but no gluttony.

The busiest libraries will contain the histories
of the forgotten, the slave, the poor and disenfranchised,
those beaten, robbed and left for dead in a ditch,
and the few who helped them.

The history books will contain heroes, but
they'll be someone else's,
and the only metanarrative will be God's.
       This will be hard.

There will be colors but no racism, sexes but no sexism,
order but no classism, languages but no imperialism.

There will be no gerrymandering of scriptures to elevate
a flag or nation, for there will be no flags or nations,
or scriptures to elevate them.
       This will be hard.

Every treasure will be buried again, and
every riddle, including this one,
explained.

There will be work but no oppression, goals
but no ambition, gain but no possession.
       This will be hard.

There will be no system of wealth and the importance
and power based on it. This will be the hardest thing
for some, and many will demand a refund
from their religion on the spot.

Money will not rule political parties because
there will be no political parties
or money to rule them.

Nothing will ever be eaten in which one must suffer
and die that another may flourish. Happiness
will never again be the result of a zero-sum game.
                                        This will be hard.

There will be no right to bear arms for private protection
or to repel all enemies foreign and domestic, for 'enemies,
foreign and domestic' will cease to be, except
as outdated terms in the Encyclopedia of Unreason.
Some will experience shock and awe when their weapons
are fashioned into symbols of peace.

There will be no deportation
of undeserving immigrants,
for that
        would
                empty
                        heaven.

There will be lands but no fences, space
but no distance, favor but no preference.
                                    This will be hard.

Everyone will have access to pure, life-giving water.

Things will begin with a great feast that will feature
someone else's food, guests that will be someone else's friends,
dress will be based on someone else's styles,
and conduct will respect someone else's mores;
and the only metanarrative
                                    will be God's.

Sachem

> "And while I stood there I saw more than I can tell, and I understood more than I saw; for I was seeing in a sacred manner the shapes of things in the spirit, and the shape of all shapes as they must live together like one being."
> - Black Elk (1863-1950)

and then, holy man took me on a canoe trip.
He helmed the boat and hummed a chant,

while the wind's strings tightened and thrummed,
and waves of pre-Columbian memory

gently gargled each metered scull.
He sighed tales of the wilderness

before the guns,
before the germs and steel and guns,

as we knifed through the liquid sun
toward a distant hump that broke

the surface like a great turtle.
Our skiff sifted light and came

to rest on crumbs of shell
in shot of autumn's chilly skeletons.

We walked beneath their moss-draped bones
frozen in perpetual shrugs

as if to ask: *Why are you here?*
Let us lodge here a while, he said,

and do what we came to do.
Did he hear them, my silver-haired

Sachem with the lean muscled frame
of the hunter-gatherer, when

all I heard was brittle wind?
Wordlessly he taught the secret

of fire, nurtured creation's breath
gathered in the hearth of the people,

and in their light we saw
as we are seen. He taught such things

not known by grasping gods and men:
things that can belong to none and meant

by all to share. There, rooted cross-legged
to the earth, I heard more of worth

within our silent hoop than all
the nations' thunder loose.

Under a million dancing tongues
of flame I came to know

how one becomes a human being.
He has passed on, my Sachem,

through the liquid sun, my Sachem.
For days in the day's darkening dusk,

the sun's blood stains a mourning sky,
and the tears of its passing mingle with mine,

until morning comes and I sail
for that place where I first became

a human being, humming the chant
to the wind's thrum and the metered sculls.

Of Parts and Partings

There's the arrival.
It's the one time
most of us will ever
be treated like a head
of state, complete
with motorcycle escort.

There's the line,
accordion
in anguished discordance
waiting turns to share condolences
and disparate memories,
like pointillism, none complete,
but together a painting.

There's the encomiums,
like a bride's veil lifted
for that binding kiss
to seal the one promise
that cannot be broken.

There's the partings
like soil plowed for sowing
seed and zippered shut,
and we finally submit
like farmers
to the mercy of seasons.

There's the gathering,
as with the opaline moon
we rise, up,
up to the podium of stars,
stand confident
as exclamation marks
and speak, every word
a kaleidoscope of light.

ABOUT ATMOSPHERE PRESS

Atmosphere Press is an independent, full-service publisher for excellent books in all genres and for all audiences. Learn more about what we do at atmospherepress.com.

We encourage you to check out some of Atmosphere's latest releases, which are available at Amazon.com and via order from your local bookstore:

In The Village That Is Not Burning Down, poems by Travis Nathan Brown

Mud Ajar, poems by Hiram Larew

To Let Myself Go, poems by Kimberly Olivera Lainez

I Am Not Young And I Will Die With This Car In My Garage, poems by Blake Rong

Saints of Sacred Madness, poems by Crystal Wells

I Would Tell You a Secret, poems by Hayden Danksy

Aegis of Waves, poems by Elder Gideon

Footnotes for a New Universe, poems by Richard A. Jones

Streetscapes, poems by Martin Jon Porter

Feast, poems by Alexandra Antonopoulos

River, Run!, poems by Caitlin Jackson

Poems for the Asylum, poems by Daniel J. Lutz

Licorice, poems by Liz Bruno

Etching the Ghost, poems by Cathleen Cohen

Spindrift, poems by Laurence W. Thomas

ABOUT THE AUTHOR

Ruben Rivera has a PhD in Religious Studies from Boston University. He recently retired after nearly 25 years as an educator at Bethel University in Saint Paul. The last six years he was Vice President for Diversity, Equity and Inclusion. The "Shalom Seminar" he created has been called a "new paradigm" in faith-based diversity efforts and reconciliation across racial and other divides.

CPSIA information can be obtained
at www.ICGtesting.com
Printed in the USA
LVHW021927160622
721465LV00004B/413